Because I could not stop.......

Minaz Ladhani Navodiya

Presentation by *BookLeaf Publishing*

Web: www.bookleafpub.com

E-mail: info@bookleafpub.com

ISBN: 9789357212014

First edition 2023

DEDICATION

"I have found the paradox,

That if you love until it hurts,

There can be no more hurt, only more love."

Mother Teresa

ACKNOWLEDGEMENT

People who bring lights are magic makers,
They shift the world and challenge you,
Break you open and inspire you.
They are your people,
They are your tribe.

Thank you for supporting me ♥♥ …..

The Divine

My divine, your colour is beautiful!
In my being, it is you,
In my entire universe, it is you.
I am nothing without you.
You celebrate the festival of colours with me,
Your colour is unique.
I admire your vivid creation.
The colour of your love is unique.

Love for Nature

The mountains are mighty and strong,
The rivers flow like my thoughts,
The ocean is deeper like the love in my heart,
The stars twinkle like my eyes,
The forests are my peace.
The exalted beauty of nature fills my soul with
the songs of gratitude.

Mesmerizing Rain

Life is full of beauty.
Listen to the rhythm of falling rain!
Pleasure is to smell the rain!
Don't wait for the storm to pass;
Learn to dance in the rain.
Some feel free not caring to get wet,
Some feel the rain, others just get wet.
It's like love,
When our souls are ready;
To rivet we feel the rain.

Rainbow: The colour of Life

Rainbow! The majestic beauty of God!
I thank Him and nod.
Enrapturing my soul,
As if His art is served in a bowl!
I feel a magic happening in the world,
So beautiful, so glorious that my heart swirled.
Admiration in my eyes for the almighty, for
creating such a magnificent universe.
The rainbow fills our lives with colours.

The Wind

What is the wind whispering?
Over the mountains during the spring.
Let the wind blow,
Where there is a black crow,
Sitting and waiting for his mate,
Who is unusually late!
The wind might have blown him far - far away,
Off to the hills or to the bay.
Someday the wind will bring him back,
And to the wind they will thank!

Mother: The Ocean of Love

Dear mother, I cannot thank you enough for the
things you have done for us!
The times you were awake just to keep us safe.
Being unwell makes me think of you now,
How you used to stay around!

The tests of life have been easier with you,
Not sure what would I do without you!
You're my strength in every length,
Regaining my pieces when I am shattered.

You are my friend when the life is bend,
You guide and love me when no one can.
I wish you are blessed with healthy life,
And be my mentor in all my strife.

Dear mother, I cannot thank you enough for the
things you have done for us!

Barren Mother

You are a mother with or without a baby!
Let the people talk who are gabby.
Giving birth doesn't make you a mother,
Hard work and responsibilities are required
further.
You do not need to be a biological mother to
love them!
Consider all the kids as a gem.
Not being able to bear a child can be agonizing,
When they say, "why don't you consider a
baby?"
Oh! What a shame! And then emanates my
profanity.
But you're fortunate in a way!
Spread your love as a spray.
You shouldn't get disheartened;
By what others say!
Calm yourself and pray.
Count your blessings,
Even without your offsprings.

Godmother

Sometimes a teacher can touch your life,
Like you have done to me,
Investing your heart in teaching.
You helped me to learn and to grow,
With your patience and wisdom, I was guided
with many more,
To bring out the best in me.
Considering how far I have come,
Being so dumb!
Your love was the key to my success,
You are a "Bless"!
And a ray of light in my dim world.

Prayers for You....

I hope you are loved,
I hope life is simpler for you, as you have
deserved.
May your world be brightened by loving and
soft words,
May you feel the radiance of joy inwards.
Let your heart be blessed with satisfaction,
Let your love be the ocean.

Dear Childhood

The child in me is calling the child in you.
Let's go and be alive, let's again live our life.
The game of hide and seek, long walks towards
the creek.
We used to boast the stories of ghosts and got
lost with our toasts.
The dolls we played with, cheered the
neighbouring kith.
The sweets we ate inside the garden gate.
The fights we had, the laughs we shared,
And at some moments we were scared.
I wish we could be the same throughout, but in
life we move out.
We change, the time changes and we have each
other in our memories.
All stays with us the whole life, I reminisce
about our childhood, with teary eyes!

A wish for a Friend!

I wish I could help you,
I wish you overcome your despair!
I wish you find someone to understand you;
I wish you find someone to alleviate your
problems.

Dear friend,

I want the best for you!
Your dismay agonises me.
I wish you can vanquish all your difficulties;
And be healthy and happy again!

If you feel you're losing everything,
Remember, trees lose their leaves every year,
And still, they stand tall;
And wait for better days to come.

Talk to someone? Who?

No one to go to,
No one to talk to.
Missing a friend who is there for you!
Not judging you!
Trust only few,
As no one is true.
Pictures of my bestie and my crew,
Feeling deserted is what I do…..

If you leave me....

If you leave me, I will be a winter without snow,
A spring without flowers,
A rainbow without colours,
A day without sun,
A night without stars,
The ocean without waves,
The beach without sand,
A fire without flames,
A book without words.
O my love, please don't leave me in dejection!

You....

The music of my soul is you,
The dance of my body is you.
The happiness I feel is you,
The peace I have is you.
You are my gravity who pulls me more and more
towards you,
I cannot keep my eyes off you.
Your dark flashing eyes magnetize me,
I find my solace in you.

Aapke Jaane ka Darr....

Aap ruthe ruthe rahte ho,
Kya baat hai jo humse chupaate ho?

Humari tanhaiyo me bhi aapka ehsaas hai,
Aap ke ruth jaane se kaha ye saans hai?

Humse pyaar karna hi aap ka kaam hai,
Wahi karne se katrate ho?

Aap ko na dekhe to dharkan ruk jaati hai,
Par is baat ka aapko ehsaas bhi hai?

Sapno me aate ho, kabhi hasaa kar kabhi rula kar
chale jaate ho.
Darr lagta hai aapko khone ka, par kaash ye darr
aap mebhi hota to baat kuch aur hoti…..

Sapno me bhi aap me simat kar rote hai,
Darte hai jab aap kehte ho, "nahi hai tujme wo
baat…."

Itna pyaar kiya wo sab khaak me mil gaya!
Khudko aap ke naam kiya aur aap kehte ho, "tu
meri nahi!"

Aap ke gale lag kar raat bhar roye, is darr se ke
aap chor kar na chale jaao.
Sapno me bhi chor kar chale jaane ki baat kehte
ho……

Teri Jogan

Teri ye berukhi humen gawaara nahi,
Is tarah baar baar dil tutna humen bardaash
nahi…..
E sanam tera yun thukra kar chale jana humen
manzur nahi.

Kabhi milo to ese milna ke har pal pyaar kiya,
Kabhi milo to ese milna ke ankhon se izhar kiya.
Nazren na chura lena tum, nazron ko nazron se
takrane dena,
Ankhon se pyaar barsa kar hume bhigo dena…..
E sanam tera yun thukra kar chale jana humen
manzur nahi.

Shayad humare pyaar me hi kami thi,
Jo har baar taklifo se guzare tum,
Warna pyaar me to wo taaqat hai,
Jo musibat me bhi tere hone ke ehsaas se jine ki
raah dikhata hai.
E sanam tera yun thukra kar chale jana humen
manzur nahi.

Jaane wale ko koi nahi rok sakta,
Shayad pyaar tha jo manata tha.

Ab us hi ki kami hai jo meri aankhon me nami
hai……
E sanam tera yun thukra kar chale jana humen
manzur nahi.

Tere pyaar ne humko sawaara hai,
Ab mil kar bichar jana humko gawaara nahi.
Tere pyaar me magan ghumti hai teri ye
jogan…..
E sanam tera yun thukra kar chale jana humen
manzur nahi.

A Hope

I have waited for you from centuries and taking
rebirths just to be with you.
Don't you realise; you have always been mine?
And now when I have found you, you are
leaving me in desolation!
I am all into you, I am born for you,
And I know one day you will come back to me,
To be with me forever and ever......

My Promise

Maybe I loved you in another life,
And have promised to find you on the other side.
You may have always been there,
In my subconscious mind,
Nudging me here and pulling me there.
Until I found you!
I don't know anything else….
But I do know that I've felt you more than one
life should allow,
And have always known you even before we
met.
Look! I've kept my promise!
Here we are together again, in this life and many
more……

Scared to Love

I have found you after a long time,
I am scared to love you this time,
Scared that you will walk away again like the
last time.
Scared to give you my all, just to find myself
shut out again this time.

Dance like nobody is watching….

Dance like nobody is watching,
Dance like you are hop scotching.
Dance is a way to be alive,
No matter what; you will thrive.
Dance makes your life merrier, or it will be
jejune!
You can dance in your own croon.
It's the drive and passion that makes you a
dancer, it's an expression of your heart.
Don't let it die within, hold on and embark!

Dance to your own tune….

Embrace the uniqueness in you!
Let the world judge you.
They haven't walked in your shoes,
Whatever you do is always news.
They haven't led your life,
They haven't faced what you have;
They never pay your debts.
Be strong!
Life comes around once,
Do what makes you happy!
Sometimes it's ok to be dappy.
You'll be criticized anyway.
Prioritize your style;
And be around those who make you smile!

9 789357 212014